To

_____

From

_____

Words
to Warm
Your Heart

DEVOTIONAL

Ellie
Claire

gift & paper expressions

Ellie Claire® Gift & Paper Expressions
Franklin, TN 37067
EllieClaire.com
Ellie Claire is a registered trademark of Worthy Media, Inc.

Words to Warm Your Heart
© 2016 by Ellie Claire
Published by Ellie Claire, an imprint of Worthy Publishing Group, a division of Worthy
Media, Inc.

ISBN 978-1-63326-152-5

Stock or custom editions of Ellie Claire titles may be purchased in bulk for educational,
business, ministry, fundraising, or sales promotional use. For information, please e-mail
info@EllieClaire.com

Cover and interior design by Gearbox Studio | www.studiogearbox.com

Printed in China

2 3 4 5 6 7 8 9 HAHA 21 20 19 18 17 16

Contents

• • • • • • • • • • • • • •

The Most Beautiful Things

· · · · · · · · · · · · · · ·

May God give you eyes to see beauty
only the heart can understand.

The best and most beautiful things in the world
cannot be seen or even touched.
They must be felt with the heart.

H E L E N   K E L L E R

You are God's created beauty and the focus
of His affection and delight.

JANET L. SMITH

Isn't it a wonderful morning?
The world looks like something God
had just imagined for His own pleasure.

LUCY MAUD MONTGOMERY

*Taking joy in life
is a woman's best cosmetic.*

ROSALIND RUSSELL

Beauty puts a face on God. When we gaze at nature,
at a loved one, at a work of art, our soul immediately
recognizes and is drawn to the face of God.

MARGARET BROWNLEY

As God's workmanship, we deserve to be treated,
and to treat ourselves, with affection and affirmation,
regardless of our appearance or performance.

MARY ANN MAYO

My mouth is filled with your praise,
declaring your splendor all day long.

PSALM 71:8 NIV

In all ranks of life the human heart
yearns for the beautiful, and the
beautiful things that God makes
are His gift to all alike.

HARRIET BEECHER STOWE

God has a wonderful plan for each person....
He knew even before He created this world what
beauty He would bring forth from our lives.

LOUIS B. WYLY

One cannot collect
all the beautiful shells on the beach.
One can collect only a few, and they are
more beautiful if they are few.

ANNE MORROW LINDBERGH

A strong positive mental attitude will create more
miracles than any wonder drug.

PATRICIA NEAL

*I've never seen a smiling face
that was not beautiful.*

Surely goodness and mercy shall follow me
All the days of my life;
And I will dwell in the house of the LORD
Forever.

PSALM 23:6 NKJV

Today a new sun rises for me;
everything lives, everything is animated,
everything seems to speak to me of my passion,
everything invites me to cherish it.

ANNE DE LENCLOS

You should clothe yourselves...with the beauty
that comes from within, the unfading beauty
of a gentle and quiet spirit,
which is so precious to God.

1 PETER 3:4 NLT

Beauty without virtue is a flower without perfume.

Something deep in all of us yearns for God's beauty,
and we can find it no matter where we are.

SUE MONK KIDD

Blessings Are Extraordinary Gifts

· · · · · · · · · · · · · · · ·

Some blessings—like rainbows after rain
or a friend's listening ear—are extraordinary gifts
waiting to be discovered in an ordinary day.

Strength, rest, guidance, grace, help, sympathy, love—
all from God to us! What a list of blessings!

EVELYN STENBOCK

Lift up your eyes. Your heavenly Father waits to bless
you—in inconceivable ways to make your life
what you never dreamed it could be.

ANNE ORTLUND

All the way my Saviour leads me—
What have I to ask beside?
Can I doubt His tender mercy,
Who through life has been my guide?
Heavenly peace, divinest comfort,
Here by faith in Him to dwell!
For I know, what'er befall me,
Jesus doeth all things well.

FANNY J. CROSBY

When you grant a blessing, O Lord,
it is an eternal blessing!

1 CHRONICLES 17:27 NLT

I will let God's peace infuse every part of today.
As the chaos swirls and life's demands
pull at me on all sides, I will breathe in
God's peace that surpasses all understanding.
He has promised that He would set within me
a peace too deeply planted to be affected by
unexpected or exhausting demands.

Let God's promises shine on your problems.

CORRIE TEN BOOM

I must exchange

whispers with God

before shouts with the world.

LYSA TERKEURST

May your footsteps set you upon
a lifetime of love.
May you wake each day with His blessings
and sleep each night in His keeping,
and may you always walk
in His tender care.

*Add to your joy
by counting your blessings.*

God has not promised sun without rain,
joy without sorrow, peace without pain.
But God has promised strength for the day,
rest for the labor, light for the way,
grace for the trials, help from above,
unfailing sympathy, undying love.

ANNIE JOHNSON FLINT

Blessed is the person who is too busy to worry
in the daytime and too sleepy to worry at night.

CAROLINE SCHROEDER

I wish I had a box,
the biggest I could find,
I'd fill it right up to the brim
with everything that's kind.
A box without a lock, of course,
and never any key;
for everything inside that box
would then be offered free.
Grateful words for joys received
I'd freely give away.
Oh, let us open wide a box
of praise for every day.

How abundant are the good things
that you have stored up for those who fear you,
that you bestow in the sight of all,
on those who take refuge in you.

PSALM 31:19 NIV

Tarry at the promise till God meets you there.
He always returns by way of His promises.

L. B. COWMAN

I will bless you
And make your name great;
And you shall be a blessing.

GENESIS 12:2 NKJV

We don't have to be perfect to be a blessing.
We are asked only to be real, trusting
in His perfection to cover our imperfection,
knowing that one day we will finally be
all that Christ saved us for
and wants us to be.

GIGI GRAHAM TCHIVIDJIAN

Sweet Contentment

· · · · · · · · · · · · · · ·

Love, consolation, and peace bloom only
in the garden of sweet contentment.

MARTHA ANDERSON

To love is to be content with the present moment,
open to its meaning, entering into its mystery.

ELIZABETH O'CONNOR

Women of adventure have conquered their fates
and know how to live exciting and fulfilling lives
right where they are. They have learned to
reinvent themselves and find creative ways
to enjoy the world and their place in it.
They know how to take mini-vacations,
stop and smell the roses,
and live fully in the moment.

BARBARA JENKINS

Contentment is not the fulfillment
of what you want, but the realization
of how much you already have.

The gentle are blessed, for they will inherit the earth....
The pure in heart are blessed, for they will see God.

MATTHEW 5:5, 8 HCSB

It is always wise to stop wishing for things long
enough to enjoy the fragrance of those now flowering.

PATRICE GIFFORD

An unhurried sense of time
is in itself
a form of wealth.

BONNIE FRIEDMAN

Where the soul is full of peace and joy,
outward surroundings and circumstances
are of comparatively little account.

HANNAH WHITALL SMITH

Be content with what you have.
because God has said.
" Never will I leave you."

HEBREWS 13:5 NIV

Let the day suffice, with all its joys and failings,
its little triumphs and defeats. I'd happily,
if sleepily, welcome evening as a time of rest,
and let it slip away, losing nothing.

KATHLEEN NORRIS

I am still determined to be cheerful and happy,
in whatever situation I may be;
for I have also learned from experience
that the greater part of our happiness or misery
depends upon our dispositions,
and not upon our circumstances.

MARTHA WASHINGTON

Our fulfillment comes in knowing God's glory,
loving Him for it, and delighting in it.

I have learned to be content
whatever the circumstances.
I know what it is to be in need,
and I know what it is to have plenty.
I have learned the secret of being content in any
and every situation, whether well fed or hungry,
whether living in plenty or in want.

Philippians 4:11-12 niv

Life is not intended to be simply a round
of work, no matter how interesting and important
that work may be. A moment's pause to watch
the glory of a sunrise or a sunset is soul satisfying,
while a bird's song will set the steps
to music all day long.

Laura Ingalls Wilder

Normal day, let me be aware of the
treasure you are. Let me learn from you,
love you, bless you before you depart.
Let me not pass you by in quest
of some rare and perfect tomorrow.

MARY JEAN IRION

The splendor of the rose and the whiteness of
the lily do not rob the little violet of its scent
nor the daisy of its simple charm.
If every tiny flower wanted to be a rose,
spring would lose its loveliness.

THÉRÈSE OF LISIEUX

Happy times and bygone days are never lost....
In truth, they grow more wonderful
within the heart that keeps them.

KAY ANDREW

Encouragement for Your Heart

. . . .

The Scriptures give us hope
and encouragement as we wait patiently
for God's promises to be fulfilled.

ROMANS 15:4 NLT

The stars exist that we might know
how high our dreams can soar.

Hope begins in the dark, the stubborn hope
that if you just show up and try to do the right thing,
the dawn will come. You wait and watch and work:
You don't give up.

ANNE LAMOTT

Moments spent listening, talking, playing,
and sharing together may be
the most important times of all.

GLORIA GAITHER

God makes our lives a medley
of joy and tears. hope. and help.
love and encouragement.

I wanted you to see what real courage is....
It's when you know you're licked before you begin
but you begin anyway
and you see it through no matter what.

HARPER LEE

For we have great joy and consolation
in your love, because the hearts of the saints
have been refreshed by you.

PHILEMON 1:7 NKJV

So when some dear joy loses
its beauteous summer glow,
Think how the roots of roses
are kept alive in the snow.

ALICE CARY

May our Lord Jesus Christ himself and God
our Father encourage you and strengthen you
in every good thing you do and say.

2 THESSALONIANS 2:16 NCV

Encouragement is being a good listener,
being positive, letting others know you accept them
for who they are. It is offering hope,
caring about the feelings of another, understanding.

GIGI GRAHAM TCHIVIDJIAN

We are so preciously loved by God
that we cannot even comprehend it.
No created being can ever know how much
and how sweetly and tenderly God loves them.

JULIAN OF NORWICH

A word of encouragement to those we meet,
a cheerful smile in the supermarket, a card or letter
to a friend, a readiness to witness when opportunity
is given—all are practical ways in which
we may let His light shine through us.

ELIZABETH B. JONES

*There are times when encouragement
means such a lot. And a word
is enough to convey it.*

GRACE STRICKER DAWSON

Calm me, O Lord, as You stilled the storm,
Still me, O Lord, keep me from harm.
Let all the tumult within me cease,
Enfold me, Lord, in Your peace.

CELTIC TRADITIONAL

Some days, it is enough encouragement just to watch
the clouds break up and disappear, leaving behind
a blue patch of sky and bright sunshine that is
so warm upon my face. It's a glimpse of divinity;
a kiss from heaven.

Every day we live is a priceless gift of God,
loaded with possibilities to learn something new,
to gain fresh insights.

DALE EVANS ROGERS

Everyone has inside himself a piece of good news!
The good news is that you really don't know
how great you can be, how much you can love,
what you can accomplish and
what your potential is.

ANNE FRANK

A Treasury of Faith

• • • • • • • • • • • • • •

In the end, I think this is what women truly desire:
to know God and to stand tall in their faith,
strong at the core, tender in heart.

RUTH SENTER

You are a child of your heavenly Father.
Confide in Him. Your faith in His love and power
can never be bold enough.

BASILEA SCHLINK

Faith means being sure of what we hope for…now.
It means knowing something is real, this moment,
all around you, even when you don't see it.
Great faith isn't the ability to believe
long and far into the misty future.
It's simply taking God at His word
and taking the next step.

JONI EARECKSON TADA

I believe in the sun even if it isn't shining.
I believe in love even when I am alone.
I believe in God even when He is silent.

Now faith is the substance of things hoped for,
the evidence of things not seen.

HEBREWS 11:1 NKJV

Only she who can see the invisible
can do the impossible.

The LORD your God is indeed God.
He is the faithful God who keeps his covenant
for a thousand generations and lavishes
his unfailing love on those who love him
and obey his commands.

DEUTERONOMY 7:9 NLT

Faith sees the invisible, believes the incredible,
and receives the impossible.

Faith is the first factor in a life devoted to service.
Without faith, nothing is possible.
With it, nothing is impossible.

MARY MCLEOD BETHUNE

God is able to take

the mess of our past

and turn it into a message.

He takes the trials and tests

and turns them into

a testimony.

CHRISTINE CAINE

I think miracles exist in part as gifts
and in part as clues that there is something
beyond the flat world we see.

PEGGY NOONAN

*Faith expects from God what is
beyond all expectations.*

Within each of us there is an inner place
where the living God Himself longs to dwell,
our sacred center of belief.

There is no unbelief;
Whoever plants a seed beneath the sod
And waits to see it push away the clod,
She trusts in God.

ELIZABETH YORK CASE

If it can be verified, we don't need faith....
Faith is for that which lies on the other side of reason.
Faith is what makes life bearable, with all its
tragedies and ambiguities and sudden, startling joys.

MADELEINE L'ENGLE

Faith is not an effort, a striving, a ceaseless seeking,
as so many earnest souls suppose, but rather
a letting go, an abandonment,
an abiding rest in God that nothing,
not even the soul's shortcomings, can disturb.

I took an inventory and looked into
my little bag to see what I had left over.
I had one jewel left in the bag,
the brightest jewel of all. I had the gift of faith.

LOLA FALANA

Let love and faithfulness never leave you;
bind them around your neck,
write them on the tablet of your heart.

PROVERBS 3:3 NIV

Faith has to be exercised in the midst of ordinary,
down-to-earth living.

ELISABETH ELLIOT

I see Heaven's glories shine,
And faith shines equal, arming me from fear.

EMILY BRONTË

The soft, sweet summer was warm and glowing,
Bright were the blossoms on every bough:
I trusted Him when the roses were blooming;
I trust Him now....

L. B. COWMAN

The Love of Family

. . . .

Family faces are magic mirrors.
Looking at people who belong to us,
we see the past, present, and future.

GAIL LUMET BUCKLEY

Home. A place where when you get there,
you know your heart has been there all along.

GLORIA GAITHER

Sooner or later we all discover that the important
moments in life are not the advertised ones,
not the birthdays, the graduations, the weddings,
not the great goals achieved.
The real milestones are less prepossessing.
They come to the door of memory.

SUSAN B. ANTHONY

Please, bless my family.
Let it continue before you always.
Lord GOD, you have said so.

2 SAMUEL 7:29 NVC

I feel from a spiritual standpoint that there's a real
celebration of humanity, of the common bond
of everybody. We need each other.

AMY GRANT

We really need only five things on this earth:
Some food, some sun, some work, some fun,
and someone.

BEATRICE NOLAN

Love allows us to live,
and through living
we grow in loving.

EVELYN MANDEL

The effect of having other interests beyond
those domestic works well. The more one does
and sees and feels, the more one is able to do,
and the more genuine may be one's appreciation
of fundamental things like home, and love,
and understanding companionship.

AMELIA EARHART

Families give us many things—love and meaning,
purpose and an opportunity to give,
and a sense of humor.

We were a strange little band of characters,
trudging through life sharing diseases and toothpaste,
coveting one another's desserts, hiding shampoo,
borrowing money, locking each other
out of our rooms, inflicting pain and kissing
to heal it in the same instant, loving, laughing,
defending, and trying to figure out
the common thread that bound us all together.

ERMA BOMBECK

What families have in common the world around
is that they are the place where people learn
who they are and how to be that way.

JEAN ILLSLEY CLARKE

When you look at your life,
the greatest happinesses are family happinesses.

JOYCE BROTHERS

We are so very rich if we know
just a few people in a way
in which we know no others.

CATHERINE BRAMWELL-BOOTH

Finally, all of you should be in agreement,
understanding each other, loving each other as family,
being kind and humble.

1 PETER 3:8 NCV

Our job is not to straighten each other out,
but to help each other up.

NEVA COYLE

Family is of the utmost importance to me. But my
family is no more perfect than [any other]....
We love, trust, get hurt, sometimes outraged,
and we love and trust anyhow,
because that's the best way to let our love grow.

MADELEINE L'ENGLE

The greatest gift we can give one another is
rapt attention to one another's existence.

SUE ATCHLEY EBAUGH

Nothing Like a True Friend

· · · · · · · · · · · · · · ·

Insomuch as any one pushes you nearer to God,
he or she is your friend.

FRENCH PROVERB

Knowing what to say is not always necessary;
just the presence of a caring friend
can make a world of difference.

SHERI CURRY

I cannot count the number of times I have been
strengthened by another woman's heartfelt hug,
appreciative note, surprise gift, or caring questions....
My friends are an oasis to me, encouraging me to go
on. They are essential to my well-being.

DEE BRESTIN

What shall I bestow upon a friend?
Gay laughter to sustain when sorrow may bring pain,
a bright song of life, a belief that winter ends
in the glory of spring, and a prayer of hope
for peace that will forever stay.

LEA PALMER

*Rich is the woman who has
a praying friend.*

JANICE HUGHES

A friend understands what you are trying to say...
even when your thoughts aren't fitting into words.

ANN D. PARRISH

Friendship is the fruit gathered from the trees
planted in the rich soil of love,
and nurtured with tender care and understanding.

ALMA L. WEIXELBAUM

Perfume and incense bring joy to the heart,
and the pleasantness of a friend
springs from their heartfelt advice.

PROVERBS 27:9 NIV

The happiest business in all the world
is that of making friends,
And no investment on the street
pays larger dividends,
For life is more than stocks and bonds,
and love than rate percent,
And she who gives in friendship's name
shall reap what she has spent.

*Thank you for the treasure
of your friendship...for showing me
God's special heart of love.*

There are some friends you know
you will have for the rest of your life.
You're welded together by love, trust, respect or loss—
or simple embarrassment.

If we would build on a sure foundation in friendship,
we must love friends for their sake
rather than for our own.

CHARLOTTE BRONTË

When you are truly joined in spirit,
another woman's good is your good too.
Your work for the good of each other.

RUTH SENTER

Don't walk in front of me—I may not follow.
Don't walk behind me—I may not lead.
Walk beside me—and just be my friend.

A friend hears the song in my heart
and sings it to me when my memory fails.

Having someone who understands is a great blessing
for ourselves. Being someone who understands
is a great blessing to others.

JANETTE OKE

We should all have one person who knows
how to bless us despite the evidence.

PHYLLIS THEROUX

I am only as strong as the coffee I drink,
the hairspray I use, and the friends I have.

A true friend is one who is concerned about
what we are becoming, who sees beyond
the present relationship and cares
deeply about us as a whole person.

GLORIA GAITHER

You Got a Gift

. . . .

There's a special kind of freedom women enjoy:
freedom to share innermost thoughts,
to ask a favor, to show their true feelings.
The freedom simply to be themselves.

Each one of us is God's special work of art.
Through us, He teaches and inspires,
delights and encourages, informs and uplifts
all those who view our lives.

JONI EARECKSON TADA

As women, we want to know we are important
and that we have a significant place in our world.
We need to know that we matter to someone,
that our lives are making a difference
in the lives of other people,
that we are able to touch their souls.
This desire to have value is God-given.

BEVERLY LAHAYE

*If your lips can speak a word of
encouragement to a weary soul,
you have a talent.*

EVA J. CUMMINGS

We know, dear brothers and sisters, that God loves
you and has chosen you to be his own people.

1 THESSALONIANS 1:4 NLT

Those who refresh others will themselves be refreshed.

PROVERBS 11:25 NLT

When I stand before God at the end of my life,
I would hope that I would not have a single bit
of talent left and could say,
"I used everything You gave me."

ERMA BOMBECK

This is the real gift: you have been given
the breath of life, designed with a unique,
one-of-a-kind soul that exists forever—
whether we live it as a burden or a joy
or with indifference doesn't change the fact that
you've been given the gift of *being* now and forever.
Priceless in value, we are handcrafted by God,
who has a personal design and plan for each of us.

WENDY MOORE

No one can arrive from being talented alone.
God gives talent,
work transforms talent into genius.

ANNA PAVLOVA

We all have different gifts, each of which came
because of the grace God gave us.... Anyone
who has the gift of serving should serve.
Anyone who has the gift of teaching should teach.
Whoever has the gift of encouraging others
should encourage. Whoever has the gift of giving
to others should give freely. Anyone who
has the gift of being a leader should try hard
when he leads. Whoever has the gift of
showing mercy to others should do so with joy.

ROMANS 12:6-8 NCV

God does not ask your ability or your inability.
He asks only your availability.

MARY KAY ASH

Every one has a gift for something,
even if it is the gift of being a good friend.

MARIAN ANDERSON

Since you are like
no other being ever created
since the beginning of time.
you are incomparable.

BRENDA UELAND

God gave me my gifts. I will do all I can
to show Him how grateful I am to Him.

GRACE LIVINGSTON HILL

Giving encouragement to others
is a most welcome gift, for the results of it
are lifted spirits, increased self-worth,
and a hopeful future.

FLORENCE LITTAUER

Lord...give me the gift of faith to be renewed
and shared with others each day.
Teach me to live this moment only,
looking neither to the past with regret,
nor the future with apprehension.
Let love be my aim and my life a prayer.

ROSEANN ALEXANDER-ISHAM

God's designs regarding you, and His methods
of bringing about these designs, are infinitely wise.

MADAME JEANNE GUYON

God Our Father

. . . .

I need not lack now any more
For any lovely thing;
I need to know my birthright for
My Father is the King!

EVELYN GAGE

Tuck [this] thought into your heart today.
Treasure it. Your Father God cares about
your daily everythings that concern you.

KAY ARTHUR

Whoever walks
toward God one step.
God runs toward him two.

JEWISH PROVERB

God is every moment totally aware of each one of us.
Totally aware in intense concentration and love....
No one passes through any area of life, happy or tragic,
without the attention of God.

EUGENIA PRICE

God is the sunshine that warms us,
the rain that melts the frost
and waters the young plants.
The presence of God is a climate of strong
and bracing love, always there.

JOAN ARNOLD

We continually recall before God our Father
the things you have done because of your faith
and the work you have done because of your love.

1 THESSALONIANS 1:3 NCV

Before anything else, above all else, beyond everything
else, God loves us. God loves us extravagantly,
ridiculously, without limit or condition.
God is in love with us...God yearns for us.

ROBERTA BONDI

As a rose fills a room with its fragrance,
so will God's love fill our lives.

MARGARET BROWNLEY

The treasure our heart searches for
is found in the ocean of God's love.

JANET L. SMITH

Nothing we can do will make the Father love us less;
nothing we do can make Him love us more.
He loves us unconditionally with an everlasting love.
All He asks of us is that we respond to Him
with the free will that He has given to us.

NANCIE CARMICHAEL

God is our merciful Father and the source
of all comfort. He comforts us in all
our troubles so that we can comfort others.
When they are troubled, we will be able
to give them the same comfort God has given us.

2 CORINTHIANS 1:3-4 NLT

The Creator thinks enough of you to have sent
Someone very special so that you might have life—
abundantly, joyfully, completely, and victoriously.

*God will never let you
be shaken or moved
from your place near His heart.*

JONI EARECKSON TADA

We do not need to search for heaven,
over here or over there, in order to find
our eternal Father. In fact, we do not even
need to speak out loud, for though we speak
in the smallest whisper or the most
fleeting thought, He is close enough to hear us.

TERESA OF ÁVILA

The God who created, names, and numbers the stars
in the heavens also numbers the hairs of my head....
He pays attention to very big things
and to very small ones. What matters to me
matters to Him, and that changes my life.

ELISABETH ELLIOT

For all these things the nations of the world
seek after, and your Father knows that you need
these things. But seek the kingdom of God,
and all these things shall be added to you.
Do not fear, little flock, for it is your Father's
good pleasure to give you the kingdom.

LUKE 12:30-32 NKJV

Stand outside this evening. Look at the stars.
Know that you are special and loved
by the One who created them.

You have the joy of this assurance—
the Heavenly Father will always answer prayer,
and He knows—just how much you can bear.

PHYLLIS HALL

A Heart Full of Gratitude

. . . .

That I am here is a wonderful mystery
to which I will respond with joy.

Enter into His gates with thanksgiving,
and into His courts with praise.
Be thankful to Him, and bless His name.

PSALM 100:4 NKJV

Give praise to the LORD, proclaim his name;
make known among the nations what he has done,
and proclaim that his name is exalted.

ISAIAH 12:4 NIV

Happiness is a healthy mental attitude,
a grateful spirit, a clear heart full of love.

If it is God who gives prayer,
then God often gives it in the form of gratitude,
and gratitude itself, when it is received
attentively in prayer, is healing to the heart.
Prayer is such a mysterious business
for something so ordinary and everyday.

ROBERTA BONDI

It is only with gratitude that life becomes rich.

DIETRICH BONHOEFFER

Appreciation is like salt—
a little goes a long way
to bring out the best in us.

Gratitude unlocks the fullness of life. It turns what we
have into enough, and more.... It can turn a meal into
a feast, a house into a home, a stranger into a friend.
Gratitude makes sense of our past, brings peace for
today, and creates a vision for tomorrow.

MELODY BEATTIE

Give thanks to the LORD, for he is good!
His faithful love endures forever.

1 CHRONICLES 16:34 NLT

I am convinced that God has built into all of us
an appreciation of beauty and has even allowed us
to participate in the creation of beautiful things
and places. It may be one way God brings
healing to our brokenness, and a way that
we can contribute toward bringing
wholeness to our fallen world.

MARY JANE WORDEN

To receive a gift, molded from love and sacrifice,
selected with care and tied up with all the excitement
the giver has to offer, is indeed rare.
They don't come along often,
but when they do, cherish them.

ERMA BOMBECK

True gratitude, like true love,
must find expression in acts, not words.

R. MILDRED BARKER

Were there no God we would be
in this glorious world
with grateful hearts
and no one to thank.

CHRISTINA ROSSETTI

Feeling grateful or appreciative of someone
or something in your life actually attracts
more of the things that you appreciate
and value into your life.
And, the more of your life that you like
and appreciate, the healthier you'll be.

CHRISTIANE NORTHRUP

Let us begin from this moment
to acknowledge Him in all our ways,
and do everything, whatsoever we do,
as service to Him and for His glory,
depending upon Him alone for wisdom,
and strength, and sweetness, and patience.

HANNAH WHITALL SMITH

Being grateful for what we have today
doesn't mean we have to have that forever.
It means we acknowledge that
what we have today is what we're supposed
to have today. There is enough....
And all we need will come to us.

MELODY BEATTIE

Influence—
the Seasoning of Life
. . . .

The blossom cannot tell what becomes of its
fragrance as it drifts away, just as no person
can tell what becomes of her influence
as she continues through life.

God's way is perfect.
All the LORD's promises prove true.
He is a shield for all who look to him for protection.

PSALM 18:30 NLT

I want just one thing.
To live long enough to pay back
in some way your undeserved
and overwhelming generosity.

PAM BROWN

*Some people make the world special
just by being in it.*

The fullness of our heart is expressed in our eyes,
in our touch, in what we write,
in what we say, in the way we walk,
the way we receive, the way we need.

MOTHER TERESA

This I learned from the shadow of a tree,
That to and fro did sway against a wall,
Our shadow selves, our influence, may fall
Where we ourselves can never be.

ANNA HAMILTON

I remember the times you were there for me,
showing real interest and concern.
I'm thankful for the closeness we share.
How I enjoy being with you!

Give, and it will be given to you. A good measure,
pressed down, shaken together and running over,
will be poured into your lap. For with the measure
you use, it will be measured to you.

LUKE 6:38 NIV

Be encouraged

in heart and united in love.

C O L O S S I A N S   2 : 2   N I V

What we feel, think, and do this moment
influences both our present and the future
in ways we may never know.
Begin. Start right where you are.
Consider your possibilities and find
inspiration...to add more meaning
and zest to your life.

ALEXANDRA STODDARD

Kind words are jewels that live in the heart
and soul and remain as blessed memories
years after they have been spoken.

MARVEA JOHNSON

Many women...have buoyed me up in times
of weariness and stress. Each friend was important....
Their words have seasoned my life.
Influence, just like salt shaken out,
is hard to see, but its flavor is hard to miss.

PAM FARREL

The real secret of happiness
is not what you give
or what you receive.
it's what you share.

Now...we ask you to appreciate those who work hard
among you, who lead you in the Lord and teach you.
Respect them with a very special love because
of the work they do. Live in peace with each other.

1 THESSALONIANS 5:12—13 NCV

Kindness is the only service that will stand the storm
of life and not wash out. It will wear well
and be remembered long after the prism of politeness
or the complexion of courtesy has faded away.

Let every woman become so cultivated and
refined in intellect, that her taste and judgement
will be respected...so unassuming and unambitious,
that collision and competition will be banished...
then, the fathers, the husbands, and the sons,
will find an influence thrown around them,
to which they will yield not only willingly but proudly.

CATHERINE BEECHER

There are two kinds of people in the world:
those who come into a room and say,
"Here I am!"
and those who come in and say,
"Ah, there you are!"

Next to God we are indebted to women,
first for life itself, and then for making it worth living.

MARY MCLEOD BETHUNE

Finding Joy

. . . .

All who seek the LORD will praise him.
Their hearts will rejoice with everlasting joy.

PSALM 22:26 NLT

Happiness comes of the capacity to feel deeply,
to enjoy simply, to think freely,
to risk life, to be needed.

STORM JAMESON

As we grow in our capacities to see and enjoy
the joys that God has placed in our lives,
life becomes a glorious experience
of discovering His endless wonders.

*There can be no happiness
equal to the joy of finding
a heart that understands.*

VICTOR ROBINSON

Where does constant joy abound?
In the restless social round,
Entertainment in excess,
Worldly charm or cleverness?
Fleeting are their seeming gains.
Joy is found where Jesus reigns.

HALLIE SMITH BIXBY

I pray that the God who gives hope will fill you
with much joy and peace while you trust in him.
Then your hope will overflow
by the power of the Holy Spirit.

ROMANS 15:13 NCV

How necessary it is to cultivate a spirit of joy.
It is a psychological truth that the physical acts
of reverence and devotion make one feel devout.
The courteous gesture increases
one's respect for others.
To act lovingly is to begin to feel loving,
and certainly to act joyfully brings joy to others
which in turn makes one feel joyful.
I believe we are called to the duty of delight.

DOROTHY DAY

Our hearts were made for joy.
Our hearts were made to enjoy the One
who created them. Too deeply planted to be
much affected by the ups and downs of life,
this joy is a knowing and a being
known by our Creator.
He sets our hearts alight with radiant joy.

A joyful heart is like a sunshine of God's love,
the hope of eternal happiness,
a burning flame of God....
And if we pray, we will become that sunshine
of God's love—in our own home,
the place where we live,
and in the world at large.

MOTHER TERESA

To be able to find joy in another's joy,
that is the secret of happiness.

GEORGE BERNANOS

When hands reach out in friendship,
hearts are touched with joy.

If one is joyful, it means that one is faithfully
living for God, and that nothing else counts;
and if one gives joy to others
one is doing God's work.
With joy without and joy within, all is well.

JANET ERSKINE STUART

You have to look for the joy.
Look for the light of God that is hitting your life,
and you will find sparkles
you didn't know were there.

BARBARA JOHNSON

Happiness is something that comes into our lives
through doors we don't even remember leaving open.

ROSE WILDER LANE

Remember: Each of us can decrease
the suffering of the world
by adding to its joy.

DAWNA MARKOVA

The LORD is my strength and my shield;
my heart trusts in him, and he helps me.
My heart leaps for joy,
and with my song I praise him.

PSALM 28:7 NIV

Laughter Is a Mini Vacation

. . . .

Take time to laugh.
It is the music of the soul.

What a circus we women perform
every day of our lives.
It puts a trapeze artist to shame.

ANNE MORROW LINDBERGH

Our mouths were filled
with laughter,
our tongues with songs of joy.

PSALM 126:2 NIV

Laughing at ourselves
as well as with each other
gives a surprising sense of togetherness.

HAZEL C. LEE

Confidence is the feeling you have before
you understand the situation.

If you don't have wrinkles,
you haven't laughed enough.

PHYLLIS DILLER

The best laughter, the laughter that can heal,
the laughter that has the truest ring, is the laughter
that flowers out of a love for life and its Giver.

MAXINE HANCOCK

This is a test. It is only a test.
If this were your actual life,
you would be given better instructions.

MYRNA NEIMS

Whole-hearted, ready laughter heals, encourages,
relaxes anyone within hearing distance.
The laughter that springs from love
makes wide the space around—
gives room for the loved one to enter in.

EUGENIA PRICE

You can't turn back the clock.
But you can wind it up again.

BONNIE PRUDEN

A cheerful look brings joy to the heart;
good news makes for good health.

PROVERBS 15:30 NLT

Sense of humor; God's great gift
causes spirits to uplift,
Helps to make our bodies mend;
lightens burdens; cheers a friend;
Tickles children; elders grin
at this warmth that glows within;
Surely in the great hereafter
heaven must be full of laughter!

People can be divided into three groups:
Those who make things happen,
those who watch things happen,
and those who wonder what happened.

Today's Forecast: Partly rational with
brief periods of coherent thought
giving way to complete apathy by tonight.

SHERRIE WEAVER

*Can it be an accident that "stressed"
is "desserts" spelled backwards?*

SUSAN MITCHELL

A good laugh

is as good as a prayer

sometimes.

LUCY MAUD MONTGOMERY

Anxiety weighs down the heart,
but a kind word cheers it up.

PROVERBS 12:25 NIV

"I wonder why people say 'Amen' and not 'A women'?"
Bobby questioned. His little friend replied,
"Because they sing hymns and not hers, silly."

Blessed are they who can laugh at themselves,
for they shall never cease to be amused.

If you can learn to laugh in spite of
the circumstances that surround you,
you will enrich others, enrich yourself,
and more than that, you will last!

BARBARA JOHNSON

Love All Around

· · · · · · · · · · · · · ·

Open your hearts to the love God instills....
God loves you tenderly.
What He gives you is not
to be kept under lock and key,
but to be shared.

MOTHER TERESA

You gave me life and showed me your unfailing love.
My life was preserved by your care.

JOB 10:12 NLT

Love is extravagant in the price it is willing to pay,
the time it is willing to give,
the hardships it is willing to endure,
and the strength it is willing to spend.

JONI EARECKSON TADA

Dear friends, let us love one another,
because love is from God, and everyone who loves
has been born of God and knows God.
The one who does not love does not know God,
because God is love. God's love was revealed among us
in this way: God sent His One and Only Son
into the world so that we might live through Him.

I JOHN 4:7-9 HCSB

*Among God's best gifts to us
are the people who love us.*

There is no need to plead that the love of God shall
fill our hearts as though He were unwilling to fill us....
Love is pressing around us on all sides like air.
Cease to resist it and instantly love takes possession.

AMY CARMICHAEL

Oh, if we did but love others!
How easily the least thing,
the shutting of a door gently, the walking softly,
speaking low, not making a noise,
or the choice of a seat,
so as to leave the most convenient to others,
might become occasions of its exercise.

MÈRE ANGÉLIQUE ARNAULD

Love...bears all things, believes all things,
hopes all things, endures all things.
Love never fails.

1 CORINTHIANS 13:4, 7-8 NKJV

Only He who created the wonders
of the world entwines hearts
in an eternal way.

Trying to find yourself within yourself
is like peeling the layers off an onion.
When you finish you have nothing
but a pile of peelings.
The only way to find yourself is to
go outside of yourself and love another.

RHONDA S. HOGAN

What we have once enjoyed we can never lose.
All that we love deeply becomes a part of us.

HELEN KELLER

Let us love so well our work shall
still be sweeter for our love,
and still our love be sweeter for our work.

ELIZABETH BARRETT BROWNING

Love grows from our capacity to give
what is deepest within ourselves
and also receive what is the deepest
within another person.
The heart becomes an ocean strong and deep,
launching all on its tide.

Nothing can separate you from His love,
absolutely nothing.... God is enough for time,
and God is enough for eternity.
God is enough!

HANNAH WHITALL SMITH

Today, see if you can stretch your heart
and expand your love so that it touches not only
those to whom you can give it easily,
but also those who need it so much.

DAPHNE ROSE KINGMA

Give Thanks and Sing Praise

· · · · · · · · · · · · · · · ·

Let us give all that lies within us...to pure praise,
to pure loving adoration,
and to worship from a grateful heart—
a heart that is trained to look up.

AMY CARMICHAEL

I will thank you, Lord, among all the people.
I will sing your praises among the nations.

PSALM 57:9 NLT

I will give thanks to the Lord
because of his righteousness;
I will sing the praises of the name
of the Lord Most High.

PSALM 7:17 NIV

I found the sun for me this morning.
I thank You, Lord.... I found the fresh air as I stood
outside the door. I praise You. For all that I see
that You do for me, I thank You. For all that
I do not see that You do for me, I praise You.

CHRISTOPHER DEVINCK

Thanksgiving puts power in living,
because it opens the generators of the heart
to respond gratefully, to receive joyfully,
and to react creatively.

Thank You, God, for little things
That often come our way,
The things we take for granted
But don't mention when we pray.
The unexpected courtesy,
The thoughtful kindly deed,
A hand reached out to help us
In the time of sudden need.
Oh, make us more aware, dear God,
Of little daily graces
That come to us with sweet surprise
From never-dreamed-of places.

Let's praise His name! He is holy, He is almighty.
He is love. He brings hope, forgiveness,
heart cleansing, peace and power.
He is our deliverer and coming King.
Praise His wonderful name!

LUCILLE M. LAW

They that trust the Lord find
many things to praise Him for.
Praise follows trust.

LILY MAY GOULD

Morning has broken like the first morning,
Blackbird has spoken like the first bird....
Praise with elation, praise every morning,
God's re-creation of the new day!

ELEANOR FARJEON

Let us always offer to God our sacrifice of praise,
coming from lips that speak his name.
Do not forget to do good to others,
and share with them, because
such sacrifices please God.

HEBREWS 13:15-16 NCV

Live today fully, expressing gratitude
for all you have been,
all you are right now,
and all you are becoming.

MELODY BEATTIE

Our thanksgiving today should include those
things which we take for granted, and we
should continually praise our God, who is
true to His promise, who has provided
and retained the necessities for our living.

BETTY FUHRMAN

Like supernatural effervescence,
praise will sometimes bubble up
from the joy of simply knowing Christ.
Praise like that is...delight. Pure pleasure!
But praise can also be supernatural determination.
A decisive action. Praise like that is...quiet resolve.
Fixed devotion. Strength of spirit.

Joni Eareckson Tada

May your life become one of glad and unending praise
to the Lord as you journey through this world,
and in the world that is to come!

Teresa of Ávila

Investing in Prayer

. . . .

Allow your dreams a place in your prayers and plans.
God-given dreams can help you
move into the future He is preparing for you.

BARBARA JOHNSON

If a care is too small to be turned into a prayer
then it is too small to be made into a burden.

We must take our troubles
to the Lord, but we must
do more than that:
we must leave them there.

HANNAH WHITALL SMITH

What God gives in answer to our prayers
will always be the thing we most urgently need,
and it will always be sufficient.

ELISABETH ELLIOT

We need quiet time to examine our lives openly
and honestly...spending quiet time alone
gives your mind an opportunity
to renew itself and create order.

SUSAN L. TAYLOR

Be kindly affectionate to one another...
fervent in spirit, serving the Lord;
rejoicing in hope, patient in tribulation,
continuing steadfastly in prayer;
distributing to the needs of the saints,
given to hospitality.

ROMANS 12:10-13 NKJV

There isn't a certain time we should
set aside to talk about God.
God is part of our every waking moment.

MARVA COLLINS

Open wide the windows of our spirits and fill us
full of light; open wide the door of our hearts
that we may receive and entertain Thee
with all the powers of our adoration.

CHRISTINA ROSSETTI

God has promised

to every single one of us

that even in our hardest times

if we would just hang on

long enough,

the blessing will come.

BETH MOORE

When we call on God,
He bends down His ear to listen,
as a father bends down to listen to his little child.

ELIZABETH CHARLES

Prayer is such an ordinary, everyday,
mundane thing. Certainly, people who
pray are no more saints than the rest of us.
Rather, they are people who want to
share a life with God, to love and be loved,
to speak and to listen, to work
and to be at rest in the presence of God.

ROBERTA BONDI

You pay God a compliment
by asking great things of Him.

TERESA OF ÁVILA

The center of power is not to be found in
summit meetings or in peace conferences.
It is not in Beijing or Washington or
the United Nations, but rather where a
child of God prays in the power of the Spirit
for God's will to be done in her life,
in her home, and in the world about her.

RUTH BELL GRAHAM

I thank my God every time I remember you.
In all my prayers for all of you,
I always pray with joy.

PHILIPPIANS 1:3–4 NIV

It is when things go wrong,
when good things do not happen,
when our prayers seem to have been lost,
that God is most present.

MADELEINE L'ENGLE

God has heard me;
He has attended to the voice of my prayer.

PSALM 66:19 NKJV

Prayer is a long-term investment,
one that will increase your sense of security
because God is your protector.
Keep at it every day, for prayer is
the key of the day and the bolt of the evening.
God is waiting to hear from you.

BARBARA JOHNSON

Priorities and Perspectives

. . . .

Time is a very precious gift of God;
so precious that it's only given to us
moment by moment.

AMELIA BARR

Our Lord does not care so much
for the importance of our works
as for the love with which they are done.

TERESA OF ÁVILA

I don't dream of wealth and success for you.
But instead, a job you like, skills you can perfect,
enthusiasms to lighten your heart,
friends, and love in abundance.

PAM BROWN

Let's not get tired of doing what is good....
Therefore, whenever we have the opportunity,
we should do good to everyone.

GALATIANS 6:9-10 NLT

The goal of much that is written about
in life management is to enable us
to do more in less time.
But is this necessarily a desirable goal?
Perhaps we need to get less done,
but the right things.

JEAN FLEMING

We need time to dream,
time to remember,
and time to reach the infinite.
Time to be.

GLADYS TABER

Life is about not knowing, having to change,
taking the moment and making the best of it,
without knowing what's going to happen next.
Delicious ambiguity.

GILDA RADNER

Forgetting those things which are behind
and reaching forward to those things which are ahead,
I press toward the goal for the prize
of the upward call of God in Christ Jesus.

PHILIPPIANS 3:13-14 NKJV

Getting things accomplished isn't nearly
as important as taking time for love.

JANETTE OKE

Be still, and in the quiet moments,
listen to the voice of your heavenly Father.
His words can renew your spirit...
no one knows you and your needs like He does.

JANET L. SMITH

We must not, in trying to think about how we
can make a big difference, ignore the small daily
differences we can make which, over time,
add up to big differences
that we often cannot foresee.

MARIAN WRIGHT EDELMAN

Live wisely among those who are not believers,
and make the most of every opportunity.

COLOSSIANS 4:5 NLT

*Never let the urgent
crowd out the important.*

KELLY CATLIN WALKER

We must know that we have been created for
greater things, not just to be a number in the world,
not just to go for diplomas and degrees....
We have been created in order to love and to be loved.

MOTHER TERESA

Choices can change our lives profoundly.
The choice to mend a broken relationship,
to say yes to a difficult assignment,
to lay aside some important work to play with a child,
to visit some forgotten person—
these small choices may affect our lives eternally.

GLORIA GAITHER

See each morning a world made anew,
as if it were the morning of the very first day;...
treasure and use it, as if it were
the final hour of the very last day.

FAY HARTZELL ARNOLD

Live each day the fullest you can,
not guaranteeing there'll be a tomorrow,
not dwelling endlessly on yesterday.

JANE SEYMOUR

Provisions—
a Heavenly Storehouse

· · · · · · · · · · ·

Focus your full attention on the goodness
and greatness of your Father rather than
on the size of your need. Your need is so small
compared to His ability to meet it.

You can trust God right now
to supply all your needs for today.
And if your needs are more tomorrow,
His supply will be greater also.

May you have warm words on a cold evening,
a full moon on a dark night,
and the road downhill all the way to your door.

*God's gifts make us truly wealthy.
His loving supply never
shall leave us wanting.*

BECKY LAIRD

Give thy heart's best treasure,
And the more thou spendest
From thy little store,
With a double bounty,
God will give thee more.

ADELAIDE ANN PROCTER

God may not provide us with a perfectly ordered life,
but what He does provide is Himself,
His presence, and open doors that bring us
closer to being productive,
positive, and realistic Christian women.

JUDITH BRILES

If God cares so wonderfully for wildflowers
that are here today and thrown
into the fire tomorrow, he will certainly care for you.

MATTHEW 6:30 NLT

God provides resting places as well as working places.
Rest, then, and be thankful when He brings you,
wearied to a wayside well.

L. B. COWMAN

I must simply be thankful, and I am,
for all the Lord has provided for me,
whether big or small in the eyes of someone else.

MABEL P. ADAMSON

A new path lies before us;
We're not sure where it leads;
But God goes on before us,
Providing all our needs.
This path, so new, so different
Exciting as we climb,
Will guide us in His perfect will
Until the end of time.

LINDA MAURICE

God will generously provide all you need.
Then you will always have everything you need
and plenty left over to share with others.

2 CORINTHIANS 9:8 NLT

It is the LORD who provides the sun to light the day
and the moon and stars to light the night,
and who stirs the sea into roaring waves.

JEREMIAH 31:35 NLT

The well of Providence is deep.
It's the buckets we bring to it
that are small.

MARY WEBB

Throughout the Bible, when God asked a man
to do something, methods, means, materials
and specific directions were always provided.
The man had one thing to do: obey.

ELISABETH ELLIOT

There will be days which are great and everything
goes as planned. There will be other days
when we aren't sure why we got out of bed.
Regardless of which kind of day it is,
we can be assured that God
takes care of our daily needs.

EMILIE BARNES

Faith is the bucket of power lowered by the rope
of prayer into the well of God's abundance.
What we bring up depends upon what we let down.
We have every encouragement to use a big bucket.

VIRGINIA WHITMAN

Simplicity

· · · · · · · · · · · · · · ·

It isn't the great big pleasures that count the most;
it's making a great deal out of the little ones.

JEAN WEBSTER

So in everything, do to others
what you would have them do to you,
for this sums up the Law and the Prophets.

MATTHEW 7:12 NIV

Silences make the real conversations
between friends. Not the saying,
but the never needing to say is what counts.

MARGARET LEE RUNBECK

Happy people...enjoy the fundamental,
often very simple things of life....
They savor the moment, glad to be alive,
enjoying their work, their families,
the good things around them.
They are adaptable; they can bend with the wind,
adjust to the changes in their times,
enjoy the contest of life....
Their eyes are turned outward;
they are aware, compassionate.
They have the capacity to love.

JANE CANFIELD

In a world where it is necessary to succeed,
perhaps...we women know more deeply
that success can be a quiet and hidden thing.

PAM BROWN

Enjoy the little things.
One day you may look back
and realize...
they were the big things.

While both boredom and serenity
address the passage of time,
the former yawns and rolls its eyes,
the latter sighs and revels in its value.

BARBARA FARMER

*It's the little things
that make up the richest part
of the tapestry of our lives.*

A fiery sunset, tiny pansies by the wayside,
the sound of raindrops tapping on the roof—
what extraordinary delight we find in the simple
wonders of life! With wide eyes and full hearts,
we may cherish what others often miss.

WENDY MOORE

Godliness with contentment is great gain.
For we brought nothing into the world,
and we can take nothing out of it.
But if we have food and clothing,
we will be content with that.

1 TIMOTHY 6:6–8 NIV

Not every day of our lives is overflowing
with joy and celebration. But there are moments
when our hearts nearly burst within us
for the sheer joy of being alive.
The first sight of our newborn babies,
the warmth of love in another's eyes,
the fresh scent of rain on a hot summer's eve—
moments like these renew in us
a heartfelt appreciation for life.

GWEN ELLIS

It is the simple things of life
that make living worthwhile,
the sweet fundamental things such as
love and duty, work and rest,
and living close to nature.

LAURA INGALLS WILDER

Don't ever let yourself get so busy that you
miss those little but important extras in life—
the beauty of a day...the smile of a friend...
the serenity of a quiet moment alone.
For it is often life's smallest pleasures and
gentlest joys that make the biggest
and most lasting difference.

The Beauty of Truth

· · · · · · · · · · · · · ·

The simplest and commonest truth seems
new and wonderful when we experience it
the first time in our own life.

MARIE VON EBNER-ESCHENBACH

Truth is the only safe ground to stand upon.

ELIZABETH CADY STANTON

Truth is always exciting.
Speak it, then.
Life is dull without it.

PEARL S. BUCK

I am amazed by the sayings of Christ.
They seem truer than anything I have ever read.
And they certainly turn the world upside down.

KATHERINE BUTLER HATHAWAY

Then Jesus said..., "If you abide in My word,
you are My disciples indeed.
And you shall know the truth,
and the truth shall make you free."

JOHN 8:31-32 NKJV

God who is goodness and truth is also beauty.
It is this innate human and divine longing,
found in the company of goodness and truth,
that is able to recognize and leap up at beauty
and rejoice and know that all is beautiful,
that there is not one speck of beauty under the sun
that does not mirror back the beauty of God.

ROBERTA BONDI

It is an extraordinary and beautiful thing that God,
in creation...works with the beauty of matter;
the reality of things; the discoveries of the senses,
all five of them; so that we, in turn,
may hear the grass growing;
see a face springing to life in love and laughter....
The offerings of creation...our glimpses of truth.

MADELIENE L'ENGLE

God does not change,

but He uses change—

to change us....

We often feel out of control,

yet if we embrace His leading,

we may find ourselves

on the ride of our lives.

JEN HATMAKER

The wonder of our Lord is that
He is so accessible to us
in the common things of our lives:
the cup of water...breaking of the bread...
welcoming children into our arms...
fellowship over a meal...giving thanks.
A simple attitude of caring, listening,
and lovingly telling the truth.

NANCIE CARMICHAEL

I have no greater joy than this: to hear that my
children are walking in the truth.

3 JOHN 1:4 HCSB

Truth is such a rare thing,
it is delightful to tell it.

EMILY DICKINSON

Amid ancient lore the Word of God
stands unique and pre-eminent.
Wonderful in its construction,
admirable in its adaptation,
it contains truths that a child may
comprehend, and mysteries into which
angels desire to look.

FRANCES ELLEN WATKINS HARPER

Every good action and every perfect gift is from God.
These good gifts come down from the Creator
of the sun, moon, and stars, who does not change
like their shifting shadows. God decided to give us
life through the word of truth so we might be
the most important of all the things he made.

JAMES 1:17-18 NCV

Open my eyes that I may see
Glimpses of truth Thou hast for me.
Place in my hands the wonderful key
That shall unclasp and set me free:
Silently now I wait for Thee,
Ready, my God, Thy will to see;
Open my eyes, illumine me, Spirit divine!

CLARA H. SCOTT

A Heart of Wisdom

· · · · · · · · · · · · · ·

Teach us to number our days,
that we may gain a heart of wisdom.

PSALM 90:12 NIV

To acquire knowledge, one must study;
but to acquire wisdom, one must observe.

MARILYN VOS SAVANT

A wise gardener plants his seeds,
then has the good sense not to dig them up
every few days to see if a crop is on the way.
Likewise, we must be patient as God brings
the answers...in His own good time.

QUIN SHERRER

The wise don't expect
to find life worth living;
they make it that way.

What we need is not new light, but new sight;
not new paths, but new strength to walk
in the old ones; not new duties
but new wisdom from on High
to fulfill those that are plain before us.

Oh, how great are God's riches
and wisdom and knowledge!
How impossible it is for us to understand
his decisions and his ways!

ROMANS 11:33 NLT

We ought to be able to learn things secondhand.
There is not enough time for us
to make all the mistakes ourselves.

HARRIET HALL

At the end of your life you will never regret
not having passed one more test,
not winning one more verdict,
or not closing one more deal.
You will regret time not spent with a husband,
a friend, a child, or a parent.

BARBARA BUSH

Live your life while you have it.
Life is a splendid gift—
there is nothing small about it.

FLORENCE NIGHTINGALE

*For the Lord gives wisdom,
and from his mouth come
knowledge and understanding.*

PROVERBS 2:6 NIV

Give generously, save consistently,
and never spend more money than you have.

MARY HUNT

I am convinced beyond
a shadow of any doubt
that the most valuable pursuit
we can embark upon
is to know God.

KAY ARTHUR